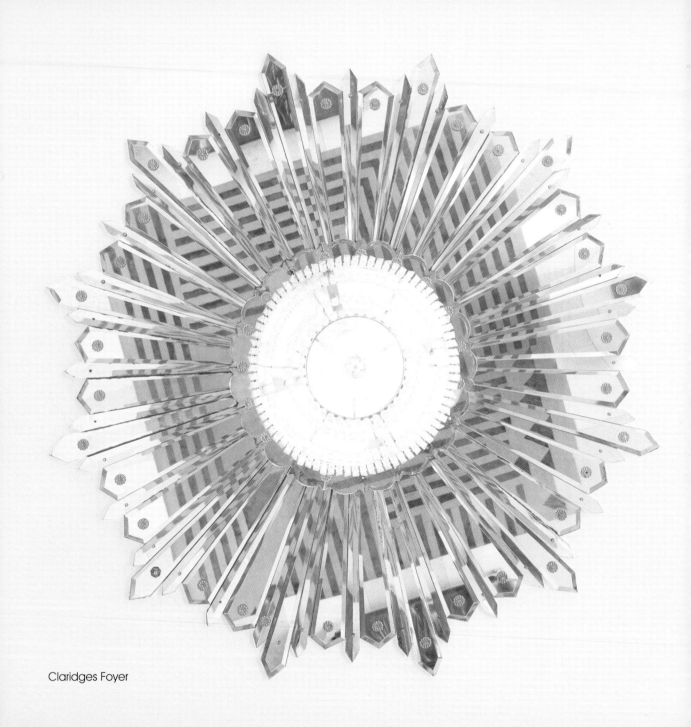

Claridges Foyer

Art Deco London

Written by Colin Hines
Photography Paul Riddle

Park House Press

Text © 2003, Colin Hines
Photography © 2003, Paul Riddle, Keith Cheetham

Art direction and design Keith Cheetham

British Library Cataloguing-in-Publication Data
A catalogue record for this book is available from the British Library

ISBN 0- 9544751- 0- 0

Published by Park House Press © 2003
PO Box 157
Twickenham
TW1 2WQ

www.artdecolondon.com

Printed by Ashford Colour Press

Front cover: Senate House
Back cover: RIBA staircase

Contents

Colin amongst his deco

Introduction

Why am I such an art deco freak? I'm convinced it all started on wintry afternoons as a child, when there always seemed to be old Fred Astaire and Ginger Rogers movies on the TV. I loved the dancing, the music, the comedy and the clothes, but the hotel rooms and sets also made an enormous impression.

It wasn't until I became a liberal studies lecturer (the last gasp of 1960s indulgence) that my good friend and sorely missed cultural mentor, the late John Morris, enlightened me about the full scope of art deco. From that moment, under the portentous guise of bringing culture to bemused skinhead gas fitters, mechanics and the like, I dragged countless groups around antiques markets, exhibitions and museums to share my enthusiasm. The Hayward Gallery's wonderful 1979 Thirties exhibition further reinforced my fixation.

My love of buildings and artefacts, films and paintings from that era has consumed me ever since. The lengths to which I will go can be attested to by my long-suffering family. I proposed to my wife, Ann, in Dolphin Square's art deco restaurant; my son, Philip, is blessed with the middle name Astaire (I have my limits, though my daughter, Clare, was spared Ginger); and we live in a marvellous curved-window, green-roof-tiled, 1935 'moderne' semi, complete with bracing draughts as the wind whistles through the panoramic Crittal windows.

Britain is losing too much of its art deco past, and the style still tends to be thought of as something mostly found abroad, in New York or Miami. This book shows where in London it still exists - places to be entertained in, to eat and drink in, to sleep in and to shop in, and to be campaigned for. The capital's deco delights range from 'palaces of the people' cinemas (many saved thanks to bingo), theatres, hotels, homes, shops and museums to even a 'decover and out' crematorium.

Hopefully *Art Deco London* will provide a tantalising glimpse of some of the best examples to please the already converted, as well as alerting many more to both London's art deco wonders and the need to preserve them. For more information visit www.artdecolondon.com

Colin Hines
March 2003

What is Art Deco?

Art deco is usually thought of as a backdrop to the luxurious and stylish lives of the wealthy in the 1920s and 1930s- huge ocean liners, jazz or big band music, the shaking of cocktails, sumptuously decorated buildings from ballrooms to cinemas, sleek cars and smooth bars. Yet this is only half the story. The reality also encompasses democratic deco, whose popular, commercial side meant that most homes boasted a curved Bakelite radio, most handbags contained a deco compact and most families enjoyed weekly visits to that high street emporium of fantasy, the cinema.

For me the defining features that make art deco such a joy are the simple curved lines, the gratifying geometric stepped shapes and the way it often breaks out into the more riotous colour and zigzag patterns so beloved of Clarice Cliff fans. One of style's most endearing characteristics can be its playfulness, verging on the kitsch. Thus a teapot could become a dashing leather-helmeted driver in a car with the registration OKT 42 (OK tea for two) and, more exotically, table lamps could be in the form of a landing female parachutist.

Amazingly, the actual term 'art deco' wasn't coined until 1966, and it wasn't until 1968 that Bevis Hillier published the first book of that title. Yet it was more than forty years earlier that the style made its first large-scale public appearance: in Paris at the 1925 Exposition Internationale des Arts Décoratifs et Industriels. The event was conceived as a celebration of modernity, bringing together the industrial and the artistic and showcasing the fresh vitality of this new approach, which ranged from architecture and interior design to fashion and jewellery. Huge international crowds visited the 150 or so pavilions, cafés, restaurants and theatres, and the result was the spread of art deco across the world.

This new architecture and design swept away the fussy ornamentation of previous centuries, replacing it with a simplicity of line influenced by the shape of machine-made objects and by expectations of an ever improving and more modern, mobile future. During the 1920s and 1930s, when art deco as a style was first in fashion, it was known as 'modernistic', 'jazz moderne' or 'style moderne'. In other words, the emphasis was on the style's modernity, not its decorative qualities. However, art deco was also inspired by historical aspects of foreign cultures and styles, from ancient Egyptian, African tribal, Central American through to the eastern exoticism of Serge Diaghilev's Ballets Russes.

Art deco was thus the first truly twentieth-century style and it was international. It has been called the last total style, since it could be utilised in the design of virtually any object, regardless of what it was to be used for or how much it cost. Art deco's emphasis on streamlining suited fast trains, luxury cars and chic 'moderne' homes. Its angular regularity suited smaller items, from cutlery to cheap brush and mirror vanity sets. Nothing has shaped, coloured and textured everyday life so extensively since. Although many of the original art deco objects were made with expensive and rare materials, new production processes and methods meant that copies could be mass-produced, so that tableware, furniture, radios, fashion and cars all reflected the style. Cinemas were the new cathedrals, adorned by regular, linear and gently curving forms.

The style has, of course, never gone away. It had its first revival in the 1960s, thanks in part to Bevis Hillier's book and events such as Biba's opening at the Kensington art deco temple of Derry and Toms. In the 1990s the MI6 building adjacent to Vauxhall Bridge faithfully replicated the detail and symmetry of the style. The Poirot deco of the TV series has also increased public interest and awareness. Art deco fairs now flourish, and because deco was the first mass-produced style, objects can still be found relatively cheaply. It will get another huge boost with this year's V&A exhibition. Let's hope this will also boost membership of the campaigning Twentieth Century Society. It is crucial that our art deco treasures be adequately protected to give future generations the chance to savour the delights of this nostalgically decadent yet fundamentally democratic style.

Cinemas | Muswell Hill Odeon

Fortis Green Road, Muswell Hill, N10

For millions in the 1930s, the cinema was where they first experienced art deco. Most famous were the Odeons, a chain created by one-time scrap merchant Oscar Deutsch. The finest surviving example of their typical house style of cream tiles, finned towers and clean, crisp lines is Muswell Hill Odeon. Designed by George Coles and opened in 1936, its 'streamline moderne' exterior style is continued inside. It has an art deco foyer, stairs to the circle and a circular light nestled in the recessed ceiling. The auditorium ceiling has elegant graduated pastel hues and an impressive illuminated ribbon running down the middle to the top of the screen.

Nearest tube: East Finchley

Cinemas | Balham Odeon

Now Majestic Wine and 'The Foyer' private lofts and flats. Balham Hill, SW12

Designed by George Coles and opened in 1938, this was a classic art deco 'streamline moderne' Odeon cinema. It closed in 1979 and the auditorium was demolished. The façade, however, was saved and the ground floor is now a Majestic Wine warehouse, while on the first and second floors there are eight apartments in an art deco style.

Nearest tube: Clapham South

Cinemas | Grosvenor Rayners Lane

Now Zoroastrian Centre for Europe
Alexandra Avenue, Rayners Lane, Harrow

Designed by F. E. Bromige and opened in 1935, this has a spectacular triple-bowed art deco frontage. Its wide central section is dominated by a huge stylised elephant's trunk with a curved 'head' at its centre. The cinema and the deco tube station opposite are now key features of the Rayners Lane Metroland conservation area. The cinema is being returned to its former splendour as the Zoroastrian Centre for Europe.

Nearest tube: Rayners Lane

Cinemas | Carlton Cinema

Now Mecca Bingo
Essex Road N1

George Coles's 1930 spectacular Egyptian revival cinema owes its survival to bingo, as do so many other such buildings. Its exterior boasts bulbous columns, stylised papyrus leaves and pyramidal forms, as well as a bold use of vividly coloured tiles. The interior is neoclassical, in a French style. Exotic cinemas like this were designed more in the 1920s than the 1930s, when the 'streamline moderne' style dominated.

Nearest tube: Highbury and Islington

Now Mecca Bingo
London Road, Hounslow, Middlesex

This simple but pleasing deco interior is typical of many cinemas all over Britain that would have ended up as piles of rubble without bingo.

Nearest tube: Hounslow East

Cinemas | Leicester Square Odeon

Leicester Square WC2

Designed by Andrew Mather and opened in 1937, this was created as the flagship for the Odeon chain. It has a black glossy granite frontage and a huge ninety-foot tower. This is still illuminated in blue neon at night and was regarded, when the building first opened, as a step towards 'night architecture'. Its art deco interior was wrecked during a crass 1960s refurbishment, although more recently there have been attempts to restore some of the detail.

Nearest tubes: Leicester Square, Piccadilly Circus

Established in 1920 as Alfredo's, this family-owned Italian café was frequented by the Krays and Mad Frankie Fraser and featured in the film *Quadrophenia*. Its magnificent chrome frontage now bears the name S&M (Sausage and Mash) and it is a licensed all-day 'community café', serving home-made British food. The café has been restored to its former glory with the help of old photographs of the original interiors.

Nearest tube: Angel

Eating & Drinking

Dick's Bar, at The Atlantic Bar and Grill,

20 Glasshouse Street, W1

Eating & Drinking

Chez Cup and The Atlantic Bar and Grill

20 Glasshouse Street, W1

Built in 1915, the Atlantic Bar and Grill is a mixture of original Edwardian and later art deco, since much of the building was remodelled in the 1930s. It has been beautifully restored, as has the adjacent Dick's Bar, a wonderful classic cocktail and champagne lounge, with its deco bar, armchairs and stunning carpet. There is also a circular private dining room, Chez Cup, with wide brown and cream lines on its wall and deco fixtures and furnishings.

Nearest tube: Piccadilly Circus

Hotels | Claridges

Brook St, WI

Five of London's major hotels, Claridge's, the Park Lane, the Dorchester, the Savoy and the Strand Palace, were built or redesigned in the late 1920s and 1930s and included outstanding art deco features in their lavish interiors. Claridge's was refurbished by Basil Ionides in the mid-1920s and by Oswald Milne in 1929-30. Its stylish art deco public areas include the elegant front entrance, built in 1930. This opens into a foyer with a stunning glass chandelier and a Lalique base beneath a deco deer etching.

Nearest tube: Bond Street

The side entrance hall contains curved art deco lights to the floor around its entrances and those of the cloakrooms. The famous tea room's décor is subtle retro deco, with a side room containing two imposing streamlined fireplaces. Around 100 rooms are still maintained in the original deco style.

Nearest tube: Bond Street.

Hotels | Park Lane
Piccadilly, W1

The rather muted silver art deco entrance on Piccadilly (not Park Lane) gives no hint that behind lies one of the most spectacular deco interiors in London. Designed by Kenneth Anns and architect Henry Tanner, the hotel opened in 1927. The entrance hall is dominated by an 'exotic-cum-neoclassical' mural and on each floor there is a magnificent staircase with a pair of wonderfully fat cylindrical stair lights set in metal work matching that on the balustrades. The breathtaking basement ballroom has stunning deco murals and other features of 1920s decoration.

Nearest tube: Green Park

Theatres | Adelphi Theatre
The Strand, WC2

The late 1920s and 1930s saw an explosion of new theatres opening in the West End, including the Adelphi, the Cambridge, the Carlton Haymarket, the Fortune, the Phoenix, the Savoy and the Saville. One of the most striking art deco façades belongs to the Adelphi. Designed by Ernest Schaufelberg and opened in 1930, the long rectangular foyer, lined with black marble, has a stepped ceiling with a huge geometric light. The dress circle bar is illuminated by the deco patterned external window and at night by a large deco angular chrome and glass light. The auditorium retains the original polished wood, marble and chrome features.

Nearest tube: Charing Cross

Designed by Edward A. Stone with interiors by Marc Henri and Gaston Laverdet, the theatre opened in 1930. Despite having been home to 'saucy' striptease queen Phyllis Dixey and Brian Rix's exuberant Whitehall farces, the theatre's exterior is very restrained, with an unadorned temple-like Portland stone façade. The interior, however, with its single balcony, contains much art deco complexity. Its black walls have silver stripes, a towering pair of art deco lamps and an octagonal ceiling design. Murals feature the mask of tragedy, musical instruments and a range of cubist designs. The rectangular stalls bar is thought to be based on an ocean liner's saloon.

Nearest tube: Charing Cross

Theatres | Cambridge Theatre

Earlham Street, Seven Dials, WC2

Designed by Wimperis, Simpson and Guthrie, and originally opened in 1930, the refurbished theatre's deco foyer has three panels of posed dancing and exercising nudes and a multilayered ceiling with concealed lighting. The interior features 'jazz age' triangular patterning by Serge Chermayeff, with brass-faced zigzag-etched inner doors.

Nearest tube: Covent Garden, Leicester Square

Situated in the basement of Austin Reed's, this relatively unknown deco treasure is reopening in the summer of 2003 as a 'grooming salon' with its original fixtures and fittings refurbished but unchanged. Designed by P. J. Westwood and completed in 1930, it was considered the most up-to-date 'tonsorial parlour' in Britain. Oval in shape, with a superb continuously undulating, wave-shaped ceiling light, it is a riot of frosted-glass zigzag deco screens, chrome, gleaming mirrors, Vitrolite walls and a Travertine marble floor.

Nearest tube: Piccadilly Circus, Oxford Circus

Shops | Barkers

Kensington High Street, W8

This department store was designed by Bernard George and opened in 1938. In many ways it looks more like a grand Odeon cinema, with its two towers of glass, but the ornamentation includes murals of chic women and store products including chairs and shoes.

Shops | Waterstone's, formerly Simpsons

Piccadilly, W1

When this shop opened in 1936 it was considered particularly stylish and well finished, with its horizontal bands of windows in large frames and its dark façade. The designer, Joseph Emberton, paid attention to such features as the lettering, the flagpole and the roof canopy, all of which add a certain deco distinction. The current owners, Waterstone's bookshop, have thoughtfully warned shoppers that the original stair rails are lower than we are used to these days.

Nearest tubes:
Piccadilly Circus, Green Park.

Public Buildings | Senate House

Malet Street, WC1

This University of London building was designed by Charles Holden and opened in 1937. Variously described as 'finely proportioned' and 'Stalinist', the Portland stone-clad stepped mass is a little reminiscent of an Aztec temple. Indeed, it tragically claimed its first sacrifice when Sir Edwin Deller, the then principal of the university, was killed when an iron container fell on him as he was inspecting the new tower in 1936. The interiors, such as the Chancellor's Hall, have classic regular proportions and are beautifully uplit. The Crush Hall has art deco wrought-iron features. A recent refurbishment has enhanced the Travertine marble walls and floors, bronze features, wood panelling and furnishings.

Nearest tubes: Euston Square and Russell Street

Public Buildings | Broadcasting House

Portland Place, W1

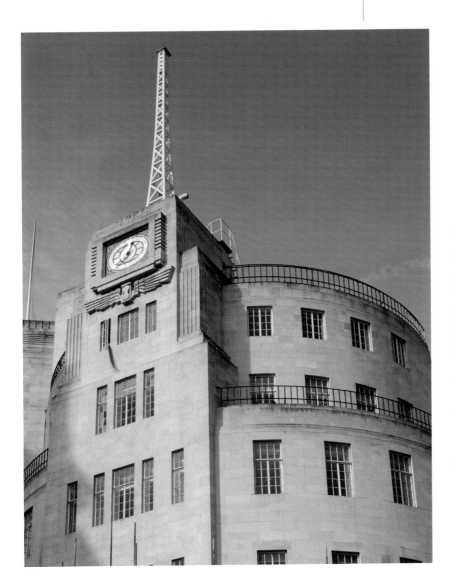

This huge, imposing flagship of British broadcasting, designed by Val Meyers and Watson, opened in 1932. Its curved Portland stone mass is studded with deco sculptural elements by Eric Gill and Vernon Hill. At its opening it was described as dividing the roadway 'like a battleship floating towards the observer'. It has a deco foyer and a restored art deco Radio Theatre, with copies of the original stepped deco lighting, carpet and original murals by Gilbert Bayes.

Nearest tube: Oxford Circus

Commercial Buildings | Hoover Factory

Now a Tesco Supermarket and Gallaher's Offices
Western Avenue, Perivale, Middlesex

Commercial Buildings | Hoover Factory

Now Tesco and Gallaher
Western Avenue, Perivale, Middlesex

Second only to cinemas in their art deco splendour are the factories of west London. Mostly built along the Great West Road, this stretch was known as the 'Golden Mile' because of its spectacular factories, each an imposing advert for its owner's products. These companies were mostly American - Firestone, Gillette, Coty, Chrysler, Packard and they built in Britain between the wars partly to avoid paying import taxes. To the north of the Great West Road on the Western Avenue is the Hoover Factory, possibly the finest art deco structure in Britain. Designed by Wallis, Gilbert and Partners, the building was their tour de force and opened in stages between 1932 and 1937. The factory has been sensitively preserved as a Tesco's supermarket, and the central office building has also been tastefully refurbished by Gallahers, keeping its original deco features. The principal building is a two-storey, low-lying white structure with its front divided into fifteen bays by massive Egyptian pillars ornately designed at the top and bottom. Its eye-catching central doorway has over the lintel a huge sunray-like design in red, blue and green, with golden arrow quills, and there are matching gates in ornate metalwork. The towers at either end have curved corner windows, sunbursts and arrow quill features. To the left of the factory is the original canteen, which resembles a streamlined Odeon cinema. Interior features include a green marble-tiled factory washroom and toilets, magnificent art deco stairways and floor-to-ceiling sunburst windows.

Nearest tube: Perivale

Commercial Buildings | Daily Express

Now Goldman Sachs
Fleet Street, EC4

Designed by Sir Owen Williams with Ellis, Clarke and Atkinson and opened in 1932, this is one of the deco landmarks of London. It has a subtly stepped, streamlined form and is clad in shiny black Vitrolite and glass. Its rounded corners are sheathed in horizontal bands of windows, alternating with polished black glass. The renowned and spectacularly striking interior was designed by Robert Atkinson. Its lighting fixtures, balustrade and other decorative and structural elements were covered in white and yellow metal. John Betjeman admiringly described it as a 'wonderful, rippling confection of metal'. No longer open to the public, it is now an office of Goldman Sachs.

Nearest tube: Blackfriars

Commercial Buildings | Daily Telegraph

Now Goldman Sachs
Fleet Street, EC4

This was designed in 1928 by Elcock and Sutcliffe with Thomas Tait, a Scot who had studied under Charles Rennie Mackintosh. Described, perhaps over-enthusiastically, as 'jazzy', the building has an imposing frontage and a huge clock. It housed offices as well as the printing plant. Now, like it neighbour the Daily Express Building, it is owned by Goldman Sachs.

Nearest tube: Blackfriars

Commercial Buildings | Imperial Airways

Now The National Audit Office
Buckingham Palace Road, SW1

This was designed by Albert Lakeman and opened in 1939. The site was chosen for its direct access to Victoria Station and thence to Southampton, where the flying boats awaited wealthy passengers. It was considered at the time to be the last gasp of London 'moderne', a huge stone structure with a concave-curved front, skyscraper stepped clock tower and, over its entrance, a pair of monumental stylised winged figures by E. R. Broadbent. Later the building served as the headquarters of BOAC and British Airways.

Nearest tube: Victoria

Commercial Buildings | Battersea Power Station

Cringle St, Off Nine Elms Lane, SW8

This was designed for the London Power Company by Sir Giles Gilbert Scott and J. Theo Halliday. The first half of the station was completed in 1934 and was described as a 'futurist icon' and a 'new cathedral'. It is now a London landmark, with its extraordinary silhouette of four fluted chimneys on stepped bases of vertically textured 'jazz moderne' bricks. What was the control room contains marvellous art deco features and Napoleon marble. Despite plans for leisure use, the site is at present derelict. Across the river is the 1930s housing development Dolphin Square, which once obtained its heating under the Thames from Battersea Power Station. Close by is another, but more common, Scott icon, a classic K2 1924-designed red telephone box. This can be viewed against the magnificent brooding backdrop of the power station.

Nearest tube: Vauxhall

Commercial Buildings | Hays Wharf

St Olaf House, Hays Wharf Company
Tooley St, SE1

This prestigious head office was designed by H. S. Goodhart-Rendel and opened in 1932. It is a unique structure, a glittering curve-edged square building on legs, clad in Portland stone. Both sides of the building have huge deco lettering and the Thames-side façade has imposing gilded ceramic figures arranged in a huge square, designed by Frank Dobson. Inside there is a classic deco staircase with zigzag balustrade and window. The building is now a private office.

Nearest tube: London Bridge

Designed by Fuller, Hall and Foulsham and opened in 1937, this beautiful, undulating, symmetrical deco building is clad in deep yellow tiles with curved corners and has an unspoilt exterior.

Nearest Tube: Aldgate

RIBA Building
Royal Institute of British Architects
Portland Place, W1

Etched
Glass

Commercial Buildings | RIBA Building

Royal Institute of British Architects
Portland Place, W1

Designed by Grey Wornum, the building was opened in 1934. The Portland stone façade is austere and symmetrical, relieved by a giant central window above bronze doors that are flanked by two pillars, one with a man and one with a woman on top.

Inside there is an impressive, wide but muted deco staircase, and the first floor café surrounded by etched glass and superb carvings is without doubt London's best authentic lunchtime deco venue, with an excellent bookshop and library.

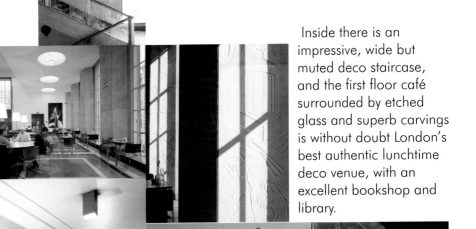

Nearest tubes: Regent's Park , Oxford Circus

Commercial Buildings | Daimler Garage

Now McCann-Erickson office
Herbrand Road, WC1

An imposing deco building designed by Wallis, Gilbert and Partners in 1931, it bears some less flamboyant similarities with their later Hoover Building, particularly with its large curved windows. It originally stored Daimler-owned cars and up to 500 privately owned cars in a garage with electrically operated pressure washing plant, waiting room and attendants office. It has recently been tastefully refurbished as offices for McCann-Erickson.

Nearest tube: Russell Square

Travel | Victoria Coach Station

Buckingham Palace Road, SW1

A rarely recognised, but nonetheless imposing art deco entrance is balanced by a wrap around exterior. It was designed by Wallis, Gilbert and Partners and opened in 1932. The interior is less impressive although its facilities were praised at its opening as warm, light, cheerful and draught-free by the doubtless more hardy, less critical customers of the day.

Nearest tube: Victoria

Travel | London Underground Headquarters

55 Broadway, SWI

Frank Pick, director of London Passenger Transport Board, wanted well designed, appealing tube stations. The result was London Underground stations designed in a futuristic Moderne manner in the 20's and 30's, mostly under the direction of Charles Holden. By 1930, Holden had full responsibility for designing more new stations having designed the London Passenger Transport board headquarters in 1926-9.

Travel | London Underground Headquarters

55 Broadway, SWI

This Portland stone, multi-stepped high-rise building was when it opened in 1929 the tallest building in London. Its almost overbearing monumentality is offset by what was considered the adventurous use of 'daring for their day' ornamental sculptures by Jacob Epstein, Eric Gill and the young Henry Moore. The latter's rather well endowed young boy in the 'Day' sculpture on the Broadway side of the building resulted in public outrage and Moore being forced to take one and a half inches off the 'prominence of the nudity'. This and the twin sculpture 'Night' were condemned on the grounds of 'obscenity, bestiality and cannibalism'. The reception area has many art deco features as does the original shopping mall that still links the exits of St James Park Underground station.

Nearest tube: St James Park

Travel | Arnos Grove

Bowes Road, N14

As part of a government public work programme the Piccadilly line was extended from Finsbury Park to Cockfosters in 1930. The distinctive 'house-style' developed by Charles Holden was applied to all the new stations built in the thirties. They included a tall, flat roofed ticket hall, with huge glass metal framed windows and often surrounding walls of red-brown bricks.

Considered the perfect Holden station, it has a drum shaped ticket hall and the original deco curved ticket purchasing and collecting booth, known as a passimeter. Although this is no longer used it has been restored to its original condition. Floodlights on the roof of the passimeter illuminated the interior at night.

Travel | East Finchley

Great North Road, N2

This Northern line Holden station is special for its huge deco archer, sculpted by Eric Aumonier. Its purpose was to represent the local ancient hunting grounds as well as a direct and speedy electric train journey into London where its arrow points.

Homes | Florin Court

Charterhouse Street, EC1

Art deco houses and flats were mostly owned by the rich or members of the middle classes, although there was some municipal rented housing built in the style. This section looks at examples of both middle- and upper-class properties. Florin Court, designed by Guy Morgan and Partners and opened in 1936, is an impressive deco apartment block, and the fictional home of the TV detective Hercules Poirot. It has an undulating exterior and a roof garden, and in the 1980s a retro deco basement swimming pool was built. Unfortunately, the deco foyer was tiled over in the 1980s.

Nearest tube: Farringdon

Homes | Author's 'Miami in Middlesex'
Moderne Semi

Apricot with a green stripe, this 1935 'moderne' semi has the typical green roof tiles and wall-length Crittal metal windows with their distinctive curved glass corner. It is part of what was originally a symmetrical road of such curved bays with 'suntrap' metal windows. The curvaceous forms and smooth white-painted surfaces gave the houses a clean, bright and, for the day, ultra-modern appearance. They had stepped-brick details on either side of wooden deco-style doors.

Living | Eltham Palace

Court Road, SE9

| # Eltham Palace
Court Road, SE9

The ultimate in wealthy deco is to be found at Eltham Palace. Stephen and Virginia Courtauld moved into their 'home' in 1936, a modern, elegant residence adjoining the Great Hall of the medieval royal palace. The art deco entrance hall, illuminated by a glazed dome, contains a sumptuous five-piece suite, table and spectacular circular carpet. The dining room has an aluminium-leafed ceiling with bird's-eye maple walls. The magnificent bathroom has a gold-leaf backdrop to an onyx bath. Throughout the house there is an 'ocean liner' feel, with veneered walls and built-in furniture.

Open 10am-6pm Wed-Fri and Sun, earlier closure in winter, closed 23rd December - 1st Feb. Telephone 020 8294 2548 for details.

Nearest tubes: Charing Cross, Victoria (then thirty minutes by train to Eltham)

One of the museum's series of reconstructed period rooms is a combined living and dining room in an art deco London flat that was built around 1935 for middle-class residents. The modernist interior has furniture kept to a minimum, with pale, plain colours. Large, wide-armed easy chairs and settees face the green marble and black slate fireplace. The rug in front of the fire provides a splash of colour and pattern in an otherwise muted room. On either side of the fireplace low shelves and cupboards provide storage space as well as display surfaces for a few carefully chosen objects. The deco dining table and chairs are compact and unobtrusive.

Admission free. Open Tuesday - Saturday 10am - 5pm
Telephone 020 7739 9893

Nearest tube: Old St, exit 2, then bus 243

Civil Engineering | Twickenham Bridge

Twickenham Road, Middlesex

Built in 1933 of reinforced concrete. Few motorists dashing round the A316 Richmond bypass realise they are passing over an excellent example of 'Egyptian deco', with concrete sunray designs, and green stepped balustrade and street lamps.

Nearest tube: Richmond

Health | Royal Masonic Hospital

Now Ravenscroft Park Hospital
Ravenscroft Park, W6

Many public buildings in the 1930s were designed in the art deco style. Without doubt one of the least well-known but most spectacular examples is Ravenscourt Park Hospital, originally the Royal Masonic. Designed by Sir John Burnet, Tait and Lorne, it was opened in 1933 when it was described as 'probably the country's largest building so far in which the spirit of modern design has been completely followed through from conception to the smallest detail'. No expense was spared. The cladding is of handmade dark red bricks and at the rear are massive and impressive tiered curved balconies ('sun balconies'). The fifty-foot-high entrance hall is breathtaking deco, with a huge floor-to-ceiling window etched with the figure of the god Aesculapius, surrounded by the signs of the zodiac. Up a magnificent marble deco staircase are two wood-panelled conference rooms with huge curved stone fireplaces.

Nearest tube: Ravenscourt Park

Health | Royal Masonic Hospital

Now Ravenscroft Park Hospital
Ravenscroft Park, W6

Decover & Out | Mortlake Crematorium

Kew Meadow Path, off Townmead Road, Richmond

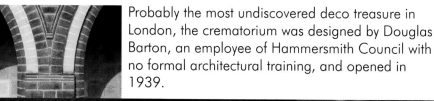

Probably the most undiscovered deco treasure in London, the crematorium was designed by Douglas Barton, an employee of Hammersmith Council with no formal architectural training, and opened in 1939.

'Hacienda deco' in style, it looks as if it belongs more in New Mexico than Mortlake. Its wealth of deco features include a wonderful chapel, iron grilles, subtle brickwork and entrance pillars and gates. At its opening, Lord Horder, the king's physician, perceptively commented, 'You seem to have eliminated the sombreness of atmosphere which sometimes shrouds buildings such as these.'

Nearest tube: Kew Gardens

RETRO DECO

Art deco had its first major revival in the 1960s, personified by the Biba style, when the trendiest women's clothes shop of the time moved into the old Derry and Toms department store in Kensington and designed clothes and products to match. Two post-war buildings that owe much to the style are the headquarters of Monsoon and the MI6 building. The Ritz has also recently opened a stylish deco Rivoli Cocktail Bar. Art deco fairs (www.artdecofairs.com) sell original deco goods, but many retro deco lamps, fixtures and furnishings are now increasingly available.

Monsoon Headquarters. Harrow Road, W2. Designed by Bicknell and Hamilton in 1968.

Nearest tube: Paddington

MI6 Headquarters. Vauxhall Cross, Albert Embankment, SE11. Designed by Terry Farrell and opened in 1993.

Nearest tube: Vauxhall

'AND NOW ITS TIME FOR A DRINK'

The Rivoli Bar, The Ritz
Piccadilly, W1

Designed by Tessa Kennedy and opened in 2001, this is a meticulous, atmospheric evocation of an elegant deco cocktail bar with wood veneer walls, Lalique glass panels and deco rugs. As such a fitting venue to drink to the future of Art Deco London.

Nearest tube: Green Park

SAVING ART DECO | THE TWENTIETH CENTURY SOCIETY

To prevent a repeat of such sad sights as the propped-up remains of the façade of the Minimax Factory in west London, it is vital that existing art deco buildings are protected. It should therefore be a priority for deco fans to support the Twentieth Century Society's campaigns to preserve the best buildings in Britain built from 1914 onwards. Initially formed in 1979 as the Thirties Society, its first big project was to ensure the prompt listing of more inter-war buildings following the shameful demolition in 1980 of the art deco Firestone Factory. Through its lobbying, conferences, tours and publications, the Society has helped save many deco and post-war buildings. It was instrumental in persuading the Tate Gallery to move to Sir Giles Gilbert Scott's Bankside Power Station and the National Trust to take on the Hampstead home of architect Ernö Goldfinger. At present it is fighting the proposed demolition of Connell Ward and Lucas's Greenside, a Surrey 1930s modern movement house, and campaigning to stop the deterioration of many neglected lidos.

The Twentieth Century Society
70 Cowcross Street
London EC1M 6EJ
Tel: 020 7250 3857
www.C20society.org.uk

Thanks and Acknowledgements

This book could not have been produced without the help and co-operation of Reg Boorer, Keith Whitbread, Dennis Gilbert, Leslie Levene, Tony Marriner, James Matthews of the Muswell Hill Odeon, the Zoroastrian Centre for Europe, Mecca Bingo, Lorraine Rossdale of the Atlantic Bar and Grill, Kevin Finch of S&M, Ellen Span of Claridges, Natasha Rhymes of the Park Lane Hotel, Mike Townshend of 'Really Useful Theatres', Craig Prentice of the Whitehall Theatre, Cynthia Barlow of Senate House, Stan Johnston of Gallaher, Bill Barron of London Underground Headquarters, Melanie Mayfield of RIBA, Ray Buckland of Florin Court, Cathy Houghton of Eltham Palace, Nancy Loader of Geffrye Museum, Helen Banks, Matron, Ravenscourt Park Hospital, Bob Coates of Mortlake crematorium, Gerrie Pitt of the Ritz.

Colin Hines is an environmentalist and former head of Greenpeace International's economic unit. Author of *Localization: a global manifesto*, he campaigns for the protection and rebuilding of local economies, whilst adequately protecting the environment. His personal 'environmental' obsession is the need for more appreciation and protection of art deco, and this book was conceived as a contribution towards that end.

Keith Cheetham began his career in television as a production designer for BBC Television working on a wide range of productions in the fields of light entertainment, drama, music and arts. He now works as a Music and Arts producer and director in film, television and theatre.

Paul Riddle worked with leading architectural photographers for a number of years and is now established as a photographer in his own right.

Daily Express interior photograph, page 34 © Angelo Hornak
Austin Reed photograph, page 27 © Peter Aprahamian
Rivoli Bar photograph, page 58 © The Ritz Hotel
Photographs of Eltham Palace © English Heritage
Photographs of Geffrye Museum © Geffrye Museum
Photographs pages 2/6/8/9/10-26/28-32/34-49/54-55/57 © Paul Riddle
Photographs pages 8/9/33/53/56/59 © Keith Cheetham